August, 2013
To Sawyer,
We hope you find ducks everywhere you go.

Love,
Aveela & Kaleb & David & Louis

The LIFE CYCLE of a DUCK

Andrew Hipp
Photographs by Dwight Kuhn

The Rosen Publishing Group's
PowerKids Press™
New York

For Mickey—Andrew Hipp
For Madisen—Dwight Kuhn

Published in 2002 by The Rosen Publishing Group, Inc.
29 East 21st Street, New York, NY 10010

First Edition

Book Design: Michael Caroleo and Michael de Guzman
Project Editor: Emily Raabe

The author gratefully acknowledges Frank Iwen for many thoughtful comments on an earlier draft of this book.

Photo Credits: All photos © Dwight Kuhn.

Hipp, Andrew. The life cycle of a duck / Andrew Hipp.
        p. cm. — (The life cycles library)
Includes bibliographical references (p.   ).
  ISBN 0–8239–5868–X (lib. bdg.)
  1. Ducks—Life cycles—Juvenile literature. [1. Ducks.] I. Title.
  QL696.A52 H566 2002
  598.4'1—dc21

                                                                00–013038

Manufactured in the United States of America

Contents

1 Finding a Mate   5

2 Tending the Eggs   6

3 Inside the Eggs   9

4 Hatching   10

5 The First Day   13

6 The Hazards of Youth   14

7 Dabbling and Diving   17

8 Molting   18

9 Tame Ducks, Wild Ducks   21

10 Moving Away   22

Glossary   23

Index   24

Web Sites   24

Finding a Mate

Ducks usually begin their **courtship** in late winter. Male ducks, or **drakes**, try to get the females' attention by **displaying** for them. They bob their heads up and down. They fluff up the feathers on their heads. They grunt and whistle, then shake their beaks and throw water into the air. A duck and drake stay together for several months. A drake fights off other males while he is with his mate, but he usually leaves about a week after his **mate** lays eggs.

◄ *In warm areas of the country, ducks may mate year-round. In the North, ducks search for a mate in November or December.*

Tending the Eggs

In March or April, the female duck finds a hidden spot of ground. She scrapes the ground with her feet and pulls leaves and grass in to make a soft nest. She lines the nest with **down** from her breast. Then she lays eight to twelve eggs, one per day. She holds the eggs against her warm breast for a month. When she leaves to eat or drink, the duck covers her eggs with down to keep them warm and hide them from crows, foxes, raccoons, snakes, and other **predators**.

In this nest, the down that is keeping the eggs warm came from the mother duck's breast. ▶

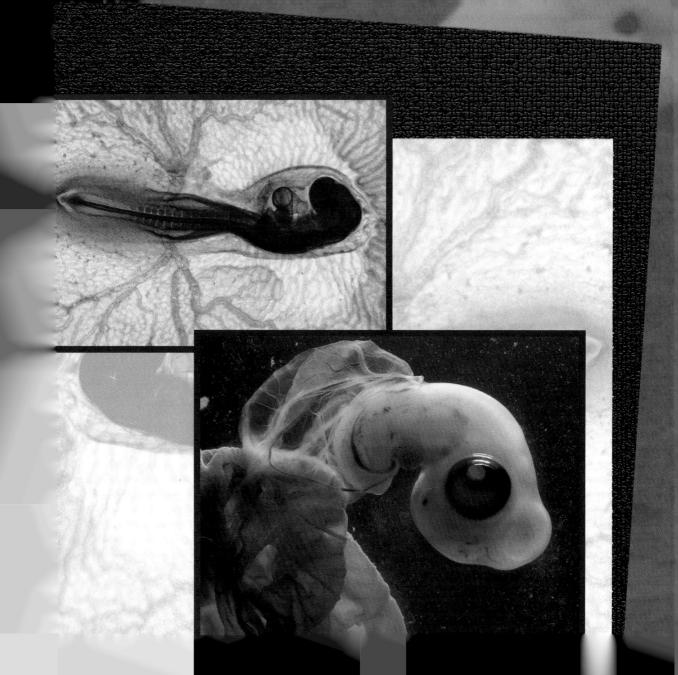

Inside the Eggs

A duck's eggshell has tiny holes that are too small to see without a microscope. These holes allow the **embryo** to breathe while inside the egg. By the fourth day, the embryo's heart is working. Two days later, it has eyes, and by the tenth day, it has ears. A fourteen-day-old embryo already has feathers! The egg yolk shrinks as the embryo takes food from it. The eggshell gets thinner as **calcium** is used up to make the embryo's bones. The embryo grows inside the egg for a month.

◀ Top Left: *This duck embryo is only 44 hours old.*
Bottom Right: *This embryo is about 5 days old.*

Hatching

At the end of a month, the duckling gets restless inside its egg. It begins to move its feet and head. As the duckling moves, a tiny, sharp **egg tooth** at the tip of its beak scrapes against the shell. The egg tooth scratches and pokes, making holes and grooves in the shell. Finally the shell breaks and the duckling comes out, wet and very tired. The eggs in a single **clutch** usually hatch within hours of each other. The egg tooth falls off a few days after hatching.

Hatching is hard work that may take from 16 to 24 hours. ▶

The First Day

The mother duck covers new hatchlings with her wings and body. The first day after hatching, the hatchlings may go for little walks outside of the nest. If the weather is bad, they stay in the nest for two or three days. When all the ducklings have rested and are ready, their mother leads them away from the nest. They are going to the water, where they will grow up. The ducklings will not return to the nest where they were born.

◄ *The hatchlings come out of their eggs wet, but they dry out within 2 to 6 hours.*

The Hazards of Youth

Young ducklings do not yet have the feathers that they need to fly. The mother must watch them carefully, because they are **vulnerable** to predators. A snapping turtle might drag one of the ducklings beneath the surface of the water. A snake or fox might grab a duckling. Even a big fish might dine on baby duck! Luckily, ducklings grow quickly. Eating seeds, roots, insects, and plant leaves helps the babies grow strong and big in a short time.

Ducklings are strong swimmers and are good at getting their own food. ▶

Dabbling and Diving

Many ducks get their food by **dabbling** their beaks in the water. They may tip their tails in the air and put their heads under the water to nibble plants, roots, and insects. They may also go onto land to eat seeds, or filter water through their bills to get insects. Other ducks dive below the water's surface for food. Dabbling ducks will sometimes dive to escape predators or to eat. Dabblers float well, however, so they can't stay underwater for very long.

◀ Top: *Some ducks dabble for food.*
Bottom: *Ducks have large feet that work like paddles, pushing them through the water.*

Molting

Birds replace all of their feathers once or twice a year in a process called **molting**. Molting allows ducks to change color. Brightly colored feathers attract the attention of mates for the ducks. Dull colored feathers help ducks to hide from predators. Molting is also a way to replace feathers that are worn out from flying. For about a month in the summer, adult ducks cannot fly, because their flight feathers are molting. During that time, they stay out of sight of predators and watch their ducklings.

At 17 days old, these ducklings are already losing their baby feathers and beginning to grow adult ones. ▶

Tame Ducks, Wild Ducks

The photographs in this book show one kind of duck, the Pekin duck. Farmers raise Pekin ducks for food. Other kinds of ducks are raised for their eggs, their down, or their meat for eating. Pekin ducks are related to the world's most common kind of wild duck, the mallard. There are more than 225 kinds of wild ducks in the world. More than 60 of them live in North America. You can see many kinds of ducks on ponds and slow rivers.

◀ *Pekin Ducks have been on farms in America since the 1870s.*

Moving Away

In the fall, many wild ducks **migrate** south for the winter. They fly in large flocks, using the sun, stars, and a view of the ground to find their way. It takes ducks several weeks to fly to their wintering ground. They rest for a few days at a time and fly when the weather is good. Ducks spend the winter eating and resting for the return trip. In the spring, they fly north again in huge flocks, returning to the same areas where they have been mating and feeding for years. Look up toward the sky during spring or fall. You may see wild ducks migrating.

Glossary

calcium (KAL-see-um) A hard mineral that is an important part of bones, teeth, and eggshells.

clutch (KLUCH) Eggs laid and cared for by a single bird at one time.

courtship (KORT-ship) The act of forming a bond between oneself and a possible mate.

dabbling (DA-bling) Splashing or dipping in the water.

displaying (dih-SPLAY-ing) Making a show to get attention. Displays may be used in courtship or to threaten another animal.

down (DOWN) A layer of small, soft, warm feathers.

drakes (DRAYKS) Male ducks.

egg tooth (EGG TOOTH) A spine at the end of a bird's bill or turtle's snout, used to break out of the shell in hatching.

embryo (EM-bree-oh) An animal or plant before it is born, when it is still in the egg, womb, or seed.

mate (MAYT) A partner for making babies. Also, to make babies.

migrate (MY-grayt) To move from one place to another.

molting (MOLT-ing) The process of shedding and replacing skin, feathers, or an exoskeleton.

predators (PREH-duh-terz) Animals that kill other animals for food.

vulnerable (VUL-ner-uh-bul) Unable to defend oneself.

Index

B
beak(s), 5, 10, 17

C
clutch, 10
courtship, 5

D
dabbling, 17
displaying, 5
down, 6, 21
drakes, 5
duckling(s), 10, 14, 18

E
egg(s), 6, 9, 10, 21
egg tooth, 10
embryo, 9

F
feathers, 5, 9, 14, 18
flying, 14, 18, 22

H
hatching, 10, 13
hatchlings, 13

M
mallard, 21
molting, 18

N
nest, 6, 13

P
Pekin duck, 21
predator(s), 6, 14, 18

W
wild ducks, 21, 22

Web Sites

To learn more about ducks, check out these Web sites:

www.kiddyhouse.com/Farm/ducks.html

www.utm.edu/departments/ed/cece/ducks.shtml

Reptiles

KINGFISHER

a Houghton Mifflin Company imprint
222 Berkeley Street
Boston, Massachusetts 02116
www.houghtonmifflinbooks.com

First published in 2006
2 4 6 8 10 9 7 5 3 1
1TR/0606/PRSP/RNB/140MA/F

LIBRARY OF CONGRESS CATALOGING-IN-PUBLICATION DATA
Weber, Belinda.
Reptiles / Belinda Weber.—1st ed.
p. cm.—(Kingfisher young knowledge)
Includes bibliographical references and index.
1. Reptiles—Juvenile literature. I. Title. II. Series.
QL644.2.W43 2006
597.9—dc22 2005031658

ISBN-13: 978-07534-5982-9
ISBN-10: 0-7534-5982-5

Senior editor: Simon Holland
Coordinating editor: Caitlin Doyle
Designer: Jack Clucas
Cover designer: Poppy Jenkins
Picture manager: Cee Weston-Baker
DTP coordinator: Catherine Hibbert
DTP operator: Claire Cessford
Production controller: Jessamy Oldfield
Proofreader: Catherine Brereton

Printed in China

Acknowledgments
The publishers would like to thank the following for permission to reproduce their material. Every care has been taken
to trace copyright holders. However, if there have been unintentional omissions or failure to trace copyright holders,
we apologise and will, if informed, endeavor to make corrections in any future edition.
b = bottom, c = center, l = left, t = top, r = right

Photographs: cover Ingo Arndt/Naturepl.com; 1bc Alamy/FLPA/Chris Mattison; 3bc Jurgen & Christine Sohns/FLPA; 4–5c Corbis/Rod Patterson;
6–7bl Getty Images/Marvin E. Newman; 7t Getty Images/Jeffrey L. Rotman; 7crb Kingfisher/Art Bank; 8b Photolibrary.com/OSF/Tui De Roy;
9tr Photolibrary.com/OSF/Mark Hamblin; 9cl Corbis/Frank Lukasseck; 9br Photolibrary.com/OSF/Robin Bush; 10cl NHPA/Daniel Heuclin;
10–11cl Corbis/Michael & Patricia Fogden; 11br Cyril Ruoso/JH Editorial/Minden Pictures/FLPA; 12bl Getty Images/Richard Coomber; 12–13t Yossi
Eshbol/FLPA; 13b Heidi & Hans-Juergen Koch/Minden Pictures/FLPA; 14bl John Cancalosi/Naturepl.com; 15t Corbis/George McCarthy; 15bl David
Kjaer/Naturepl.com; 16b Corbis/John Conrad; 17t Getty Images/Peter Weber; 17cr Getty Images/Dr. Dennis Kunkel; 17b Corbis/Joe McDonald;
18bl Photolibrary.com/OSF; 19tr Barry Mansell/Naturepl.com; 19br Anup Shah/Naturepl.com; 20b Corbis/Nigel J. Dennis; 21t Getty Images/Paul
Chesley; 21cl Corbis/ Michael & Patricia Fogden; 21c Alamy/IT Stock Free/Dynamics Graphics Group; 22bl Tui De Roy/Minden Pictures/FLPA; 23cl Flip
Nicklin/Minden Pictures/FLPA; 23b Photolibrary.com/OSF/Tobias Bernhard; 24c Pete Oxford/Minden Pictures/FLPA; 25tr Photolibrary.com/OSF/Stan
Osolinski; 25cl NHPA/Stephen Dalton; 25br NHPA/Stephen Dalton; 26c Photolibrary.com/OSF/Ingo Arndt; 27tl Patricia & Michael Fogden/Minden
Pictures/FLPA; 27cr NHPA/Daniel Heuclin; 27br Photolibrary.com/OSF/Michael Fogden; 28b Photolibrary.com/OSF/Michael Fogden; 29cl D. Zingel
Eichhorn/FLPA; 29cr Rupert Barrington/Naturepl.com; 30b Michael & Patricia Fogden/Minden Pictures/FLPA; 31tr Getty Images/Steve Winter; 31br
NHPA/Laurie Campbell; 32b Getty Images/Bill Curtsinger; 33tl Chris Mattison/FLPA; 33cr NHPA/Martin Harvey; 34–35bc Corbis/Rod Patterson; 35tr
Getty Images/Altrendo Nature; 35br Getty Images/Theo Allofs; 36bl John Cancalosi/Naturepl.com; 37tr Photolibrary.com/OSF/Dani Jeske; 37b Getty
Images/Theo Allofs; 38bl NHPA/Anthony Bannister; 38–39c Photolibrary.com/OSF/Tobias Bernhard; 39tr ZSSD/Minden Pictures/FLPA; 39br Getty
Images/Joel Sartore; 40cl NHPA/Daniel Heuclin; 40br Still Pictures/Lynda Richardson; 40–41c Corbis/Philip Gould; 48br Getty Images/Jeff Hunter.

Commissioned photography on pages 42–47 by Andy Crawford
Project maker and photo shoot coordinator: Jo Connor
Thank you to models Dilvinder Dilan Bhamra, Charelle Clarke,
Madeleine Roffey, and William Sartin

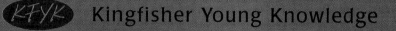

Kingfisher Young Knowledge

Reptiles

Belinda Weber

KINGFISHER
BOSTON

Contents

What is a reptile? **6**

Different types **8**

Temperature control **10**

Reptile skin **12**

Reptile senses **14**

Foot functions **16**

Fangs and teeth **18**

Moving on land **20**

Moving in water **22**

Moving in trees **24**

Finding food **26**

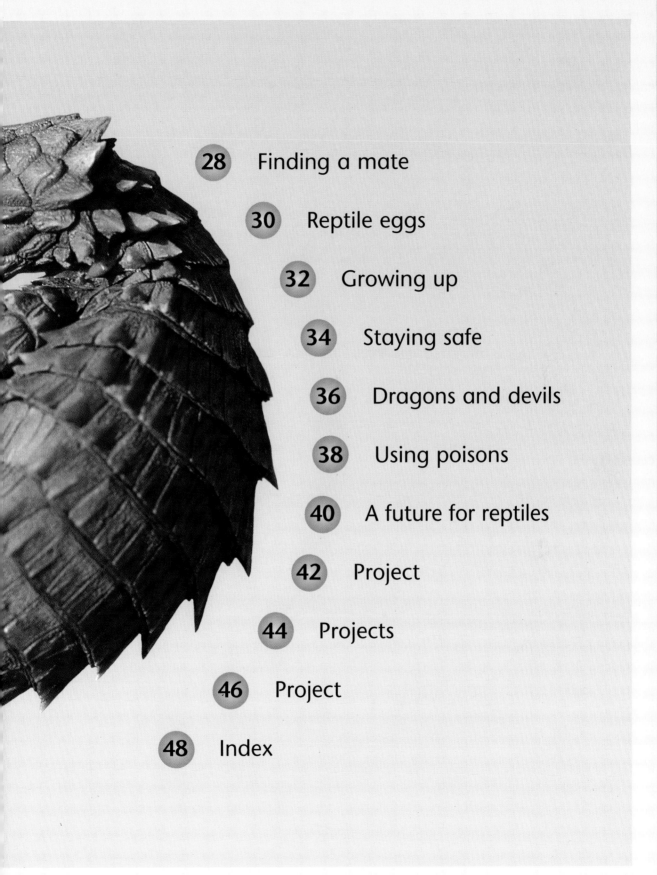

28 Finding a mate

30 Reptile eggs

32 Growing up

34 Staying safe

36 Dragons and devils

38 Using poisons

40 A future for reptiles

42 Project

44 Projects

46 Project

48 Index

What is a reptile?

Reptiles are a group of animals with tough, scaly skin. They have a skeleton and a backbone. There are more than 6,500 different types of reptiles.

Tough and scaly

Reptile skin is covered in thin, protective plates called scales and is stronger than normal skin. Alligators' skin is covered in thick, horned plates.

skeleton—the frame of bones inside of an animal's body

Water features

Crocodiles live close to water. Like waterbirds, they have webbed feet to help them swim.

Different homes

All reptiles are suited to where they live. Alligators have the correct type of body for moving both in and out of water.

Prehistoric reptiles

Reptiles have prehistoric ancestors. Archelon was a giant sea reptile that is related to modern-day turtles.

ancestor—an animal from which later animals have developed

Different types

Reptiles come in many different shapes and sizes. The largest of all are the saltwater crocodiles, which grow to around 23 feet long. Reptiles are divided into four different groups.

Reptiles with shells

Turtles, terrapins, and tortoises belong to this group. They all have hard, bony shells to protect their soft bodies inside.

species—a set of animals or plants that have the same features

Lizards and snakes

This is the largest reptile group. There are more than 3,000 different species of lizards and snakes found all over the world.

The crocodilians

Alligators, crocodiles, caimans, and gharials belong to this group. They can all move quickly on land, but most of them are found wallowing in water.

A group apart

Tuatara are the only members of the smallest reptile group. They are only found on a few small islands off the coast of New Zealand.

wallowing—lying still while floating in water

Temperature control

Reptiles are cold-blooded, which means that their bodies stay at the same temperature as their surroundings. They lie in the sun to warm up and hide in the shade to cool down. Once they are warm, they hunt for food.

Too cool to move

When some reptiles, such as rattlesnakes, find it too cold, they hibernate (go into a deep sleep) until warmer weather returns.

digest—to break down food so that the body can use it

Staying warm

Chameleons bask in the sun to warm up their blood. Reptiles need to be warm in order to hunt and digest their food.

Cooling off

A crocodile cools down by "gaping" its mouth wide-open. Or, it can take a dip in the river or lie in the shade.

Reptile skin

All animals need skin in order to keep their insides in and to stop them from drying out in the sun. Skin also helps protect the animal's insides from injuries.

Spiky skin

Some reptiles, such as iguanas, have spikes along their backs to protect them from predators. These tough scales are made from keratin.

predators—animals that hunt other animals

Smooth skin

Burrowing reptiles, such as sandfish, have smooth, flexible scales. These lie flat against the skin to help the skink slide into its burrow.

Growing bigger

A snake sheds its skin as it grows. It wriggles until it is free from its old skin. This is called sloughing.

keratin—a tough substance found in hair, claws, and fingernails

Reptile senses

Senses help animals understand their surroundings. All animals use their senses to find food, stay safe, and find a mate. Most reptiles can see, hear, and smell, and some can also "taste" things in the air.

eardrum

Listening lizards

Lizards do not have soft ears on the outside of the head like we do. They have an eardrum on each side of their head to pick up sounds.

eardrum—a part of the ear that sends sound vibrations to the inner ear

Tasting smells

Many snakes and lizards flick out their tongue to "taste" the air. A sense organ in their mouth figures out what the tastes are.

Looking all around

A chameleon can move each eye on its own. This means that the animal can look in two different directions at the same time.

organ—a part of the body with a special job

Foot functions

Reptiles exist all over the world, so they need to be able to live in many different habitats. Their feet have evolved and adapted to suit their way of living. Some climb, some dig, while others can grip onto branches.

Spreading the weight

Giant tortoises have huge feet. As they climb over sandy ground, their big feet help spread out their weight so that they do not sink.

Gripping pads

This gecko is an excellent climber. Tiny, hooklike hairs on its feet (shown on the right) allow it to cling onto almost anything.

Walking on water

Basilisks have wide feet and broad, scaly toes. They move quickly on these special feet to prevent them from sinking as they run across water.

evolved—*changed over time*

Fangs and teeth

Some reptiles are small and hunt insects. Larger ones eat meatier creatures such as mammals. All reptiles have a mouth and teeth that are suited to catching and eating their prey.

Snapping jaws
The jaws of alligator snapping turtles have sharp edges. The turtles snap them shut to slice their prey into bite-size pieces.

mammals—warm-blooded animals that feed their young on milk

Foldaway fangs

This rattlesnake has two sharp, hollow teeth called fangs, which can be unfolded for biting. Poison is pumped through the fangs to kill the prey.

Catching fish

The mouth of the Ganges gharial is lined with small, sharp teeth. The teeth fit together tightly to stop fish from getting away.

prey—*an animal hunted by another animal*

Moving on land

All reptiles have a bony skeleton that helps give their body its shape. Many reptiles have four legs, but snakes and some lizards do not have any legs at all. Most reptiles can move quickly to hunt or escape from danger.

Handling the heat

The Namib sand gecko has long legs. When it gets too hot, the gecko pushes up on its legs to lift its underside away from the scorching desert sands.

flexible—*bendable, stretchy*

Sidewinders

Sidewinder rattlesnakes wriggle and loop their bodies along the hot ground. This way, only a small part of their body touches the scorching hot sand at a time.

Inside of a snake

A snake's skeleton has a flexible backbone with ribs attached to it. It is very bendable, so a snake can coil up or wrap around things.

Moving in water

Some reptiles live in the water, while others swim in order to find food or cool themselves down. All reptiles breathe air, so even those that live in the water need to surface often to breathe air.

Finding food

Marine iguanas are the only ocean lizards in the world. They feed on seaweed and can stay underwater for around 20 minutes.

Graceful swimmers

Green sea turtles beat their front flippers like wings and use their back flippers for steering. Their smooth shells help them move through the water.

Powerful swimmers

Saltwater crocodiles swish their long tails from side to side to push them through the water. Their legs help them steer.

flippers—limbs that are suited to swimming

Moving in trees

Many reptiles are good climbers. Geckos that live in trees have special foot pads for gripping slippery leaves, while some snakes have ridged scales for clinging onto branches.

Clinging on

Tree snakes have long, strong bodies. They wrap themselves around branches and reach out into the open to look for predators or prey.

glide—to gently float through the air

Gripping claws

Monitor lizards have strong legs and feet with long claws for gripping.

Leaping lizards

The flying gecko has webbed feet and folds of skin along its sides, legs, and tail. It uses these to catch the air and glide.

Flying lizards

This flying dragon lizard has flaps of skin along its ribs, which are useful as "wings" for gliding.

Finding food

Although some lizards only eat plants, most reptiles are carnivores that hunt other animals. Some reptiles, such as crocodiles, have a varied diet, while others only eat one type of food.

Elastic tongue
Chameleons grip onto branches. They have a long, sticky tongue, which they shoot out at high speeds to catch any bugs that they see.

carnivores—animals that eat meat

Eating frogs' eggs

When the cat-eyed snake finds a cluster of frogs' eggs, it slurps up the whole sticky mass.

Leafy dinner

The Solomon Islands skink is strictly a plant eater. It climbs trees to feast on the fresh green leaves.

Fresh eggs

The African egg-eating snake swallows whole eggs. It pierces the shell in its throat, so that it does not spill.

pierce—to prick and break into

Finding a mate

When animals are ready to breed, they find a mate. Some reptiles use smell to attract a partner, while others use colors, sounds, and even dancing. Many males fight to win a female.

Bright throat

This male anole puffs up its colorful throat and nods its head up and down. This shows females that he is ready to mate and warns off any rival males.

breed—to produce babies

Breeding dance

Speckled rattlesnake males prove their strength by wrestling. They are venomous, but they do not bite each other.

Wrestling match

Using their tails for support, male monitor lizards rear up on their back legs and fight rival males. The weaker male gives up.

venomous—*poisonous*

Reptile eggs

Most reptiles lay eggs with soft but tough shells. The egg's yolk provides the developing young with food. The shell protects it from outside conditions.

developing—*growing and changing*

A turtle's nest

This olive ridley sea turtle is laying around 100 eggs into a hole that she has dug in the sand. She will return to the sea after burying them.

Breaking out

Developing snakes grow an "egg tooth" on the tip of their upper jaw. They use this to pierce the eggshell when they are ready to hatch.

Live babies

Some snakes and lizards give birth to live young. This lizard's Arctic home is too cold for eggs.

hatch—*to break out of an egg*

Growing up

Baby reptiles usually look like smaller versions of their parents. They are able to catch their own food as soon as they hatch. Some begin by eating smaller prey than the adults eat.

Digging for freedom
Newly hatched olive ridley sea turtles dig their way out of their sandy nests. They crawl as quickly as they can toward the sea.

miniature—tiny

Growth ridges

As a tortoise's shell grows, another ridge is added to the patterns. People can figure out the animal's age by counting the ridges.

ridges

Caring mothers

Although it is a fierce predator, this female Nile crocodile is also a caring mother. She gently scoops her babies into her mouth to keep them safe.

ridge—*a narrow, raised area on a flat surface*

Staying safe

Reptiles use many different tricks to stay hidden while they are hunting or resting. If they are startled, some pretend to be dead. Others show that they are poisonous by their bright colors.

Armor plating

An armadillo lizard has sharp, spiny growths on its skin. When the lizard is threatened, it grabs its tail and curls up into a spiky ball.

startled—surprised

Hiding in the leaves

Gaboon vipers have mottled patterns on their skin. This helps them stay hidden among the leaves.

Gaboon viper

Too big to eat?

Frilled lizards have a flap of skin around their heads that they can lift up. This makes them look bigger and scarier if a predator attacks them.

mottled—*patterned with different colored patches*

Dragons and devils

Lizards are the most successful group of reptiles and live in many different places. Some lizards have developed into big and fierce predators. Others are much smaller and live in trees, or even underground.

Dragons with beards

When it is threatened, the bearded dragon puffs up a spiky flap of skin under its chin. This makes it look too big to eat.

Big dragons

Komodo dragons are the largest of all lizards. They can catch goats and pigs, but they usually eat carrion.

carrion—*the dead bodies of animals*

Thorny devils

A thorny devil's spines and prickles protect the animal against attacks. They also catch dew for the lizard to drink.

dew—*small drops of water that form on grass and plants during the night*

Using poisons

Many reptiles use venom (poison) to kill their prey. Venom can affect the nervous system, the tissues of the body, or even the blood. Venomous reptiles may also use these poisons for self-defense.

Spitting cobras

A spitting cobra sprays venom out of its mouth and aims for its enemy's eyes. The poison is very painful and can cause blindness.

nervous system—*the network of nerves throughout an animal's body*

A poisonous bite

Gila monsters are one of two species of venomous lizards. Their venomous saliva (spit) poisons prey as they bite and chew.

Swimming snakes

Sea snakes are the most venomous snakes in the world. They can swim underwater for up to five hours.

Noisy rattles

Rattlesnakes twitch the loose scales at the end of their tail to make a rattling sound. This warns enemies that their bite is poisonous.

saliva—*clear liquid produced in the mouth*

A future for reptiles

Many reptiles are in danger or face extinction. We need to learn how our actions may harm reptiles and do more to take care of them.

Harmful trade

Many reptiles are killed for their skins. The skins are then used to make wallets, boots, belts, and souvenirs for tourists.

Tracking reptiles

This loggerhead turtle is being fitted with a radio transmitter. Scientists will monitor its movements so that they can learn more about this creature.

extinction—when all animals of a certain type die, and none are left

Returning to the wild

This alligator was once caught and sold as a pet. Luckily, it was rescued and returned to its real home.

radio transmitter—a device that sends out signals to be tracked

Lizard cape

Make your own frilled cape

The Australian frilled lizard defends itself by using its neck frill (see p. 35). Make one yourself to see how this special defensive system works.

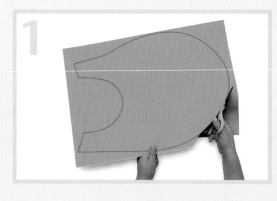

Draw one half of the frill shape onto a large sheet of colored cardboard. Use scissors to cut out the shape.

You will need
- Two large sheets of cardboard
- Pencil
- Scissors
- Tape
- Poster paints
- Paintbrush
- Colored tissue paper
- Glue
- String

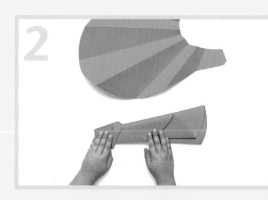

Make the other half of the frill with another sheet of cardboard. Fold each half like an accordian.

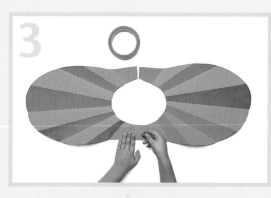

Place the two halves together and connect them using tape at one end.

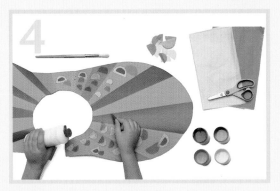

Create a pattern for your cape using paint. Cut out pieces of tissue paper and stick them on using glue to create a scaly texture.

Cut two long pieces of string. Attach them at each end of the cape—to the unpainted side—using tape.

Place the finished cape around your neck and use the string to hold it in position. Give it a pull to raise the frilly cape and scare away your enemies!

Pop-up croc

Create a greeting card
Learn how to cut and fold paper to make your very own pop-up card. Then decorate it for a friend or relative.

You will need
- Colored cardboard
- Pencil
- Scissors
- Poster paints and paintbrush

1 Fold the cardboard in half and draw a zigzag line for the teeth. Cut along the line using scissors.

2 Fold the teeth shape out, as shown, so that there is a definite crease. Unfold the cardboard so that it is flat.

3 Draw out the rest of your croc in pencil and color it in with paints. Press out the teeth to make the cardboard work.

Snake stick

Make a slinky snake toy

Snakes have a flexible backbone. Create this model, then use the stick to copy the way that a snake coils and slinks over land.

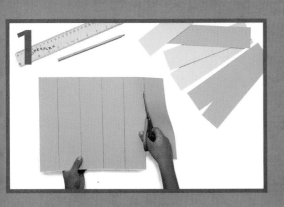

1

Use a ruler to draw equal strips onto the colored cardboard. Use scissors to cut out the strips.

You will need
- Colored cardboard
- Pencil
- Ruler
- Scissors
- Tape
- Paints
- Paintbrush
- String
- Wooden stick

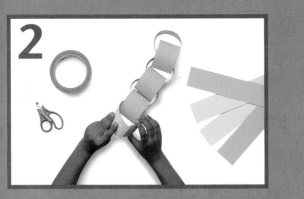

2

Using tape, make one strip into a loop. Connect the other strips on in loops. Add a pointed loop for the tail.

3

Add eyes and a forked tongue. Paint on markings. Stick one end of string close to the head and the other end to a stick.

Sticky tongues

Pretend to be a chameleon

Chameleons shoot out their sticky tongues to snatch juicy bugs (see p. 26). With this game, you can pretend to do the same!

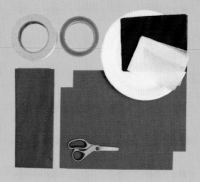

1

Roll up sheets of cardboard to make two tubes—one slightly thinner. Attach the tubes using tape. Paint the tubes red.

You will need
- Colored cardboard
- Tape
- Poster paints
- Paintbrush
- Red tissue paper
- Double-sided tape
- Black tissue paper
- White tissue paper
- Scissors

2

Fit the slightly thinner tube inside of the larger one. Use tape to hold the two tubes together.

3

Scrunch up lots of red tissue paper into a ball. Add strips of double-sided tape to make it sticky.

Push the ball of tissue paper into the end of the long tube. The double-sided tape should hold it in. This forms the tip of your sticky tongue.

Make flies by scrunching up smaller pieces of black tissue paper. Cut out wing shapes using white paper or tissue. Stick them on using tape.

Make two of these sticky tongues. Then, put all your flies into a bowl or onto a paper plate, and you are ready to play . . . The person who collects the most flies in one minute is the winning chameleon!

Index

alligators 6, 7, 9, 41
babies 30, 31, 32–33
caimans 9
chameleons 11, 15, 26–27,
   46–47
crocodiles 7, 8, 9, 11, 23,
   26, 33, 44
dragon lizards 36, 37
eggs 27, 30–31
feet 7, 16–17, 24, 25
flying lizards 25
frilled lizards 35, 42–43
geckos 17, 20, 24, 25
gharials 9, 19
Gila monsters 39
iguanas 12, 22
legs 20, 23, 25, 29
lizards 9, 11, 12, 13, 14,
   15, 17, 20, 22, 25, 26,
   27, 28, 29, 31, 34, 35,
   36, 37, 39
monitor lizards 25, 29
mouths 11, 18–19
rattlesnakes 10, 19, 21,
   29, 39

scales 6, 12, 13, 24
sea snakes 39
sea turtles 23, 31, 32, 40
senses 14–15
shells 8, 23, 33
skeletons 6, 20, 21
skin 6, 12–13, 25, 34, 35,
   36, 40
snakes 9, 10, 13, 15, 19,
   20, 21, 24, 27, 29, 30,
   31, 35, 38, 39, 45
tails 23, 25, 29
teeth 18–19
terrapins 8
thorny devils 37
tortoises 8, 16, 33
tree snakes 24
tuatara 9
turtles 7, 8, 18, 23,
   31, 32, 40